The Store Cupboard Cook Book

The Store Cupboard Cook Book

JANICE BEVERLEY BRYANT
ILLUSTRATED BY PAT FRICKER

ISBN: 1500124109
ISBN 13: 9781500124106

Contents

Recipes

Introduction

*H*aving a supply of ingredients at hand enables you to be adventurous and ready for any occasion. These days, it is almost a sin to waste food because the cost is ever increasing. This is why I am hoping to help a lot of you, whether you are single or newly married, a student, or a first-time homeowner. This book is for anyone, not forgetting members of the older generation, like myself.

Nutrition

W^{hat is a diet?}

Your diet is, quite simply, what you eat. There are two aspects of food intake: paying attention to the amount of food you eat to keep a healthy weight and making sure you consume food that is high in nutrients and vitamins to do you good.

For you to function properly, you must have an intake of both minerals and vitamins, as well as carbohydrates, protein, and fats. Having the correct ingredients at home, where you can easily balance your diet, is far better than buying fast food and ready-made meals.

I often hear friends and strangers say they can't be bothered cooking for one. "It's hardly worth it," they say. But I'm sure that with a little care and determination, they could rustle up a mid-week dinner party for two and enjoy a special meal with a friend. Often it is loneliness that causes people to lose interest in cooking.

In the past, I looked after elderly people, and many of them didn't have an appetite. I understand that caregivers are pushed for time, but I am sure one hour a week can be found to have a meal with an elderly person and talk about old times—even just a plate of thinly cut sandwiches and some homemade cake. Lay the meal on doilies; have tea in nice china cups. The effect would be so appreciated. It would give him or her something to look forward to each week, and you may also enjoy the experience. One word of caution, though: talk this plan over with the individual first. A lot of elderly people like to maintain their independence, so tread lightly.

On the plate below, you will see what your daily intake of the various food groups (veg, carbs, meats, dairy, sweets) should be.

On this plate are essential items for a healthy diet, but this is only a guide. Also use the list of store-cupboard ingredients to add different things to make a nourishing meal.

Below are two examples of a simple nourishing meal that can easily be experimented with:

1. Lay a fillet of fish on some greaseproof paper or tinfoil. Add salt and pepper, some lemon juice, chopped parsley, a knob of butter, and a couple of tablespoons of milk. Cover the fish, and cook in the oven for five to ten minutes. As an alternative, don't use foil, and cook in the microwave for less time). When removing, be cautious, as the food can get very hot. Put the cooked fish onto a warm plate, and serve with bread and butter or a small salad.

2. Cut up broccoli and cauliflower into small florets, and cook in a saucepan until almost tender. Drain and place into a small ovenproof dish. Bring some full-cream milk to the boil. Dissolve some cornstarch in a little cold milk or water, add it to the hot milk, and beat the mixture to get rid of lumps. When it is smooth, remove it from the heat

and stir in grated cheese (or red Leicester, for color). Season and pour over the cooked cauliflower. Sprinkle some cheese on top. Bake or grill so the top is golden brown. (**Note:** When preparing the dish, pour the cold milk into your ovenproof dish to about half full. This enables you to measure the amount you need before you put it into the saucepan to heat.) This is a quick and tasty meal. This can also be used with macaroni. For nonvegetarians, chop up and cook some lean bacon or gammon (preferably smoked) to add to the dish.

A lot of recipes can be made in advance and frozen or chilled in the fridge for a couple of days. If you reheat a meal in the oven, cover it with tinfoil first to stop it from drying out. You may need to add a little milk or water, especially to the macaroni dish described earlier.

Creating A Store Cupboard

A store cupboard is an important part of any kitchen. Having ingredients on hand is useful to enthusiastic cooks and novices alike.

A store cupboard can be created in any small place. Even if you live in a tiny apartment, a small shelf can be used to store a few extra items, as also a rack of dried herbs and a couple of essential kitchen gadgets, such as an eggbeater and cheese grater. If you have a bit more space, you can use large plastic boxes. These can be bought cheaply, stacked up, and slotted together. Some come with wheels attached, and they are often available in bright colors.

If you have plenty of space in your garage or utility room, you can build a cupboard. Some of us are fortunate enough to have a walk-in pantry, which affords lots of space. Whatever you have at your disposal, follow the same rules. Start small, and build up your supplies gradually.

Don't be too exotic to begin. Start by building up basic ingredients, such as flour, sugar, rice, and pasta. Each time you shop, buy one or two extra items that will add to your stock. Keep an eye on what you have in your store cupboard, and check every month for out-of-date items. Have a little notepad handy, and write down items as they are used up so you can replace them. You don't want to run out at a critical moment.

Over the years, I have enjoyed cooking, but recently, maybe like you, I have been inspired further by the skills of some of the cooks I see regularly on TV. If you're like me, you love to impress your friends with your cooking skills. Even if you live in a tiny apartment or studio and can't host a full dinner party, you can put a nice white cloth on a small table and fill it with culinary delights. Adding a good wine and some soft music will certainly set the mood. Cooking something new and tasty for either yourself or friends I am sure will make you happy. This will be possible if you have all the ingredients you need every time you look at a recipe. For bedtime reading, choose a basic recipe book. Scan through it, and make a list of some of the ingredients you may find useful.

As well as advising you on different ingredients to stock in your store cupboard, I have added little bits of history now and then that I hope you find interesting. You will also find a few recipes at the back of the book.

Lastly, a word of advice: when shopping, don't always use a supermarket. Most towns have a good market; take time out to look around. Most of the vegetables you can buy in a market are fresh and in season. It's great to serve tomatoes or strawberries at Christmas, but not if they are horrible and have no taste, which is likely to be the case, especially if you live in a cooler climate. Buying in a market or small shop is also more convenient, especially for a single person. The market will weigh up just the amount you need, which means you save money *and* food. Large amounts of prepackaged and buy-one-get-one-free offers are more suited for larger families, not for one person living alone or even a couple on a limited budget. I don't dismiss supermarket buying. In fact, supermarket prices on products like milk, butter, and margarine can't be beat. But be cautious.

It is still possible to eat cheaply but well. There is no need to cut corners; it just takes a little planning. There seems to be a cultural shift toward fast food these days. Fast food is OK on a very special occasion, if you must. But the amount you spend on these meals could feed a small family for a week.

One thing more: if you can't cook or find it boring, don't panic! Give it a try. You will likely be pleasantly surprised, especially if someone praises you for your efforts.

FILLING YOUR STORE CUPBOARD

On the next few pages, I've made a list of essential items to give you a start. Of course, if you have limited space, you won't be able to stock all of them. Look at this list as a guide. It might be a good idea to make a copy to pin up on the cupboard door. Why not make your own list according to your taste?

Starting to Fill Your Store Cupboard

arborio rice
applesauce
baking powder
barley (pearl barley)
bicarbonate of soda (aluminum-free)
baked beans
beef patties
butter beans (dried, also in cans)
biscuits
bread
bread mixes
basmati rice
cream crackers
couscous
cereals
caster sugar (a finer grain, suitable for cake making)
chicken stock cubes
coconut milk
chickpeas
cornstarch
cooking chocolate

cocoa powder

coffee

curry powder

potato chips

corned beef

dumpling mix

Dijon mustard

dried fruit (mixed fruits, dates, apricots, peaches, raisins, and currants)

desserts (packets of trifle, pudding mixes, and so on)

English mustard (dried or ready made)

eggs

frozen foods

fish paste

flour (all purpose, self raising)

garlic (fresh or dried)

granulated sugar

honey

horseradish

hot dogs

instant mashed potatoes or tinned potatoes

jam

jelly

Jaffa Cakes

ketchup

linguine

lasagna

ladyfingers

meat

macaroni

minestrone soup

milk

mandarin oranges

mayonnaise

maraschino cherries (tinned or in glass jars)

notepad and pen (to attach to door of store cupboard)

nachos

noodles

nuts

naan

olive oil

olives

oxtail soup

oats

pudding rice

pickles and chutney

pepper

pasta

peanut butter

parmesan cheese

pancake mix

rennet (for making junket)

rice pudding (tinned)

relish

rice

red kidney beans (tinned)

salt (table salt, sea salt, rock salt)

sugar (granulated, caster, brown)

semolina

sauces (tomato, brown, chili, Worcestershire)

suet

syrup (maple, golden and black treacle)

tea (green, herbal, black)

tinned fruits, fish, vegetables, rice, and tomatoes

vinegar (malt, cider, wine, balsamic)

walnuts

whole-wheat bread

wafers

yam

yogurt

zucchini

Here are a few points to remember:

- Build your store cupboard gradually.
- Each time you visit the supermarket, buy one or two extra items (e.g., baking powder, cornstarch, and so on).

- Eventually, if room allows, have two of anything that you use a lot of (e.g., tea, sugar, flour, and the like).
- Store cereals, rice, lentils, nuts, and the like in smaller plastic containers or glass jars. Label.
- Keep a notebook or weekly chart on the back of the door so you know when to replace stock.
- Watch expiration dates and shelf life. Don't worry if an item is a couple of days over. If perishable items (e.g., bacon and ham) are opened, use straightaway or within a couple of days. Use sausages the same day. If you only use half of an item, freeze the rest. Don't waste.
- Keep cans on lower shelves. They are heavy if they fall.
- When using packets, make sure to close the tops securely.
- Keep the cupboard clean and tidy at all times. You can line the shelves with shelf liners, which can be changed regularly, or paint the shelves with white gloss paint.
- Take vegetables out of plastic bags and keep in a vegetable rack for air to circulate. Unwashed potatoes last longer than washed ones.
- Cover all food in the fridge so flavors don't mingle.
- Store raw meat at the bottom of the fridge, as blood can drip onto lower shelves. After buying meat, it may be better to make it oven ready and store in a dish.
- Wash hands thoroughly in soapy water before handling food. Pay close attention to washing hands after handling raw meat and fish.
- Keep all surfaces clean. If you are on a limited budget, hot, soapy water is as good as any chemical spray. Clean ovens and fridges regularly.
- Change dishcloths and tea towels regularly.
- When handling chilies, wash hands thoroughly, or wear plastic gloves. Keep hands away from eyes.

Cereals

We all have our favorite cereal. To make sure everybody has a good start to the day, take several different types from the cupboard every morning to fill the table.

There are shelves in the supermarket full to the point of bursting with these colorful boxes, all promising health and vitality.

Cereals are convenient and quick to serve, and you can guarantee children will like most of them, which means they leave the house with a full stomach. This is especially important on cold winter mornings.

Some common cereals are porridge oats, cornflakes, muesli, and shredded wheat. All-Bran, Weetabix, Alpen, Bran Flakes, Shreddies, and Cheerios are some popular breakfast-cereal brands.

Other cereals and grains include maize, rice, wheat, barley, millet, oats, and rye.

If you only have limited space, buy only one or two favorite cereals at a time. Store them in plastic containers rather than in their original packaging.

Of course, you should avoid grains and gluten if you have celiac disease or a similar illness.

It's worth following my recipes. They are child friendly and cheaper than store-bought cereals.

Rice and Pasta

Types of Rice

Below I have listed a few types of rice that are most commonly used. Worldwide there are more than forty thousand different varieties.

Arborio rice is an Italian short-grain rice with high starch content, which is traditionally used for risotto.

Long-grain rice, or all-purpose rice, is light and fluffy. It is ideal for curry.

Brown rice is rice with the husk. It takes a bit longer to cook, is mildly nutty in flavor, and is very nutritious.

Short-grain pudding rice is for use in rice puddings.

Types of Pasta

There are many different types of pasta. Below is a list of the best-known types.

Spaghetti is a long and thin pasta, it can be prepared with meat or vegetables for a healthy meal.

Lasagna are flat sheets of pasta that can be layered with meat, vegetables, and cheese.

Linguine is flat spaghetti that is nice with wild mushrooms topped with parmesan cheese.

Penne are small cut tubes that can be used instead of spaghetti.

Cannelloni are large, hollow rolls that can be stuffed with meat or vegetables.

Ravioli are square-shaped pasta (approximately three by three centimeters) that are typically stuffed with spinach, cheese, and ground meat.

Gnocchi are dumplings made with flour and potatoes.

Couscous is a grain-like pasta common in North Africa and Europe (especially France, but becoming popular in the United Kingdom).

Macaroni is long, narrow, tube-like pasta. It is available as long strips like spaghetti, but thicker. You can also by packaged short-length macaroni, which is better for making milk puddings and macaroni and cheese.

Pasta is economical and satisfying. It is full of essential nutrients, iron, and vitamin B. Pasta provides a slow release of energy and is also high in fiber. Dried pasta should be stored in jars or plastic containers.

You can also make your own pasta. See recipe for homemade pasta below.

Fresh Pasta Dough

If you have a pasta-making machine, all the better, but good results can be achieved with a rolling pin, too.

140 g (5 oz.) plain flour (finely ground flour if possible)
2 medium eggs, 1 whole and 1 yolk

Rubbing-in method: Place all the ingredients on a flat surface, and mix in gradually with your hands. To start, it's very gooey, but it soon comes together. When the dough forms a ball shape, start to knead. Knead for at least two minutes, longer if you can manage it. When smooth, wrap in plastic wrap and place in fridge for one hour to rest.

Quick method: Put the ingredients into a food processor to bind together into fine crumbs. Don't add any water. Put onto a flat surface and knead. Let rest for one hour.

Cut the dough into two pieces. Roll out with a rolling pin until it's about a quarter inch (five millimeters) thick.

Fold over the dough into thirds, and pass it through the pasta machine. Roll seven times, until you have a rectangular shape and the dough is very thin and shiny.

Repeat with the second piece of dough. Cut into shapes. Keep all the pasta separate and well floured so it does not stick together and get tangled.

Note: Don't make too much at a time. Unless you can store it somewhere to dry, it will stick together. Homemade ravioli can be frozen. Follow the recipe below.

Ravioli
Filling ingredients

250 g or ½ lb. spinach
1 cup or 8 oz. ricotta

Cook some spinach for about two minutes. Drain and let cool. Chop it up a little, and add some ricotta cheese. Season very lightly with sea salt and black pepper. Mix in the ricotta, and set aside.

Lay half of the rolled-out pasta on a floured surface. Then with a biscuit cutter (square or round), cut the shapes out, and lay a teaspoon of the spinach mix in the center of each and brush beaten egg around the edges.

Cut some more shapes with the other half of the pasta, lay these on top, and push down the edges to seal. Spread them out on a baking tray to freeze. When frozen, they can be put into a container together for a later date.

With practice, you can lay two sheets of pasta on the flat surface and spoon the filling at regular intervals. Take up the plain sheet, lay it on top of the filling, and cut between. Again make sure the ends are sealed. Cook for two minutes in boiling water, or freeze.

When you decide to cook the pasta, make sure it goes into boiling water. Use a slotted spoon to remove when cooked. Put onto a warm dish and top with grated parmesan cheese and black pepper.

Parmesan cheese in the little boxes you can buy in the supermarket is fine. To buy a block at the cheese counter is expensive, but now and then you should treat yourself. If you store it in the fridge or freezer and grate it as you need it, it will last a long time.

Pizza Dough

1 kg bread flour (or type 00)
200 g (7 oz.) finely ground semolina flour
1 level Tbsp. fine sea salt
1 Tbsp. caster sugar
2 x 75 g sachets of dried yeast
4 Tbsp. extra-virgin olive oil
650 mL lukewarm water

Sieve all the flour and salt onto a clean work surface. Make a well in the center. Put the yeast, sugar, olive oil, and water into a jug. Let sit for a few minutes, and then pour into the well. Bring the flour gradually into the liquid with a fork, and swirl it around, mixing more of the flour into the center. Keep mixing until all the flour is used. Now start to mix the ingredients with well-floured hands. When the dough is mixed, knead for at least ten minutes, until smooth and springy.

Place the dough in a well-floured bowl, cover with a damp cloth, and store at a warm temperature a warm room is OK. When it has risen to double its size, turn it out onto a clean, dry surface. Knead the dough again; this is called *knocking back*. You can use the dough immediately or wrap in plastic and put it in the fridge or freezer to use at a later date. You can also roll it out into round, flat plates, cover with foil, and freeze.

Use your favorite topping, and bake in a hot oven (about 450°F) for about ten minutes or until it is light brown on top.

Suggested toppings: grated cheese, tomatoes, ham, anchovy, chopped pineapple (an English favorite!)

It's like an open pie, so use any topping that takes your fancy.

A Short History

Pizza was originally a street food made from bread dough to feed the poor of Naples. As time went on, toppings were added, making the bread tastier and more popular with the masses. A Neapolitan chef, Raffaele Esposito, made a pizza for the queen consort of Italy, Margherita of Savoy, and garnished it with tomatoes, mozzarella cheese, and basil to represent the colors of the Italian flag. He was honored by her.

CANNED FOOD

An army marches on its stomach.

—NAPOLEON

It was a constant struggle during the Napoleonic Wars to feed large numbers of men with fresh food. The French government of the time offered a large cash award to anyone who could come up with an effective method of preserving large amounts of food.

In 1809, Nicholas Appart, a confectioner, found that cooking food inside a sealed glass jar kept it fresh. The reason for this at the time was unknown, as it was fifty years prior to Louis Pasteur's demonstration of the role microbes have in food spoilage.

Glass food containers, however, presented challenges for transportation. Thus glass jars were replaced with canisters (shortened to *cans* following the work of Peter Durand in 1810). Cans were far less fragile and cheaper to make than glass.

Though the can opener had not yet been invented, soldiers found they could easily open cans with their bayonets.

Nutritional Value

A balanced diet consists of protein, carbohydrates, fresh vegetables and dairy.

It is often thought that food is destroyed during the canning process and will not taste as fresh. This is not the case. In fact, sometimes food that has been canned is superior to the original. Tinned tomatoes are a good example.

Canned food can be so useful as a mainstay. Having a stock of cans in the bottom of your store cupboard means a quick meal can always be had at a moment's notice. Thus canned goods are very important to have on your list of basic items. It is important, however, to check labels for salt and sugar content. Be aware, and buy reduced if possible.

Here are some tinned goods that I can recommend keeping in stock;

Soup: Soup is a good idea for a quick lunch. It can be served with crusty bread.

Baked beans: You can easily prepare beans on toast! Add an egg or top with grated cheese, and this could be a main meal if you are strapped for time.

Mixed beans: Beans come in all colors and can be mixed with a green salad in your lunch box for added protein.

Fruit: If you can buy tins of fruit in natural juice, all the better. Syrup is too sweet and not so healthy.

Vegetables: Peas, potatoes, runner beans, broad beans, and artichokes are all available in cans.

Fish: Canned fish include salmon, pilchard, tuna, mackerel, and sardines.

Pasta and rice: Spaghetti, macaroni and cheese, macaroni milk pudding, and rice pudding are additional canned items to keep in stock.

There are many different tinned foods on the market, some quite exotic. Scan the supermarket shelves to see what's available.

PERISHABLE ITEMS

If a food is labeled "perishable," that means it will deteriorate very quickly.

Storing Perishable Foods

Store raw meat in the fridge, and cook within two days. If you want to buy bigger amounts of meat, you should separate it into individual portions and store these in plastic bags or boxes in the freezer.

Fish: Fish is best eaten on the same day as purchase. It can also be frozen.

Dairy products: Milk, cream, eggs, and butter must be refrigerated. Read the expiration dates.

Fruits and vegetables: The difference between a market stall and a supermarket is the packaging. Supermarkets pack vegetables in plastic that makes them sweat, and they are usually sold prewashed, which also shortens their shelf life. Vegetables from a greengrocer or market stall are generally sold in brown paper bags, which enables air to circulate. You are also able to buy only the amount you need, small or large. Fruit is also better bought loose. Put it in a fruit dish on arriving home; it is more likely to be eaten if it is visible.

Flour

Some important information about flour

Flour is a powder made of cereal grains or roots. It is the main ingredient of bread, the staple of civilization as a whole.

There are many types of flour, but I will be covering the main types you will need in your store cupboard. As you become more ambitious, adding another type will be easy.

Flour is one of the world's most valuable and versatile foods. It is over eight thousand years old and still going strong, full of essential vitamins and minerals and a cornerstone of our diet.

Here are most of the flour types that you will be using;

Plain flour is also known as all-purpose flour. Use it for sauces where a raising agent is not required. (I make Yorkshire puddings with plain flour.)

Self-rising flour has an evenly mixed raising agent. Use it for cakes and puddings. (I use self-rising flour for pastry making.)

Strong plain flour is high in protein and has a high volume and open texture. It is ideal for bread and all types of yeast cookery.

Whole-wheat flour is 100 percent extraction—made from the whole wheat grain with nothing added or taken away.

Stone-ground whole-wheat flour is ground in the traditional way, between two stones.

Gluten-free flour is also widely available. Many people now follow this trend, mostly for health reasons. There are many books on the market covering this subject, and I recommend you read some of them. You will be pleasantly surprised.

Always use quality ingredients.

Sugar

*I*t is important to know sugar comes from several different sources, here is a short list.

It's amazing to think that the sugar we have always thought of as a product from plantations in the West Indies and other warm climates is also grown in other places. While many brown sugars, such as demerara (popular in England, nice on cereal), muscovado, dark- and light-brown sugars, and turbinado are grown in other countries, England also grows its own sugar.

For many years, East Anglia has been an English sugar plantation. Local farmers grow sugar beet and transport it to the refinery a short distance away, where it is turned into fine British sugar.

The product is manufactured with concern for the environment and an aim to reduce the carbon footprint. The heat and water from the making of the sugar is used to grow seventy million British tomatoes. Recyclable paper is used to pack the sugar when it is ready for the supermarket. How proud we can be of homegrown products! It must be good for the environment for a product not to travel halfway around the world to reach our tables.

Below is sugar used every day.

Granulated sugar is a coarse sugar for general use. It is suitable for sweetening drinks, cereals, and fruit.

Caster sugar has fine granules. It is used for baking.

Confectioners' or icing sugar is sugar that has been ground to a powder. It is used for making icing and also for sieving lightly on top of Victoria sponges or cupcakes for that professional look.

Preserving sugar is used for jam making. It contains pectin, which helps to set the jam.

Coconut palm sugar is a healthier alternative for general use and is similar to brown sugar.

Salt

There are several types of salt.

Table salt is one of the most widely used salts. It contains chemical additives.

Sea salt is available in both fine and coarse varieties. This salt includes several naturally present trace minerals, including iodine, magnesium, and potassium, all of which give the salt a fresher, lighter flavor. Less is required when cooking.

Rock salt is sold in large crystals. It has a grayish hue because it is unrefined. This salt makes a great bed for oysters and clams.

Salt is also a good antiseptic and is ideal for bathing cuts and grazes; it can even be gargled to aid a sore throat.

VEGETABLES

Along with fruit, vegetables make up part of your "five a day," so it is very important to include a variety in your diet.

Whether you grow your own or buy them, vegetables store quite well, although not for long. So don't buy in bulk unless you intend to freeze them.

Below is a list of some of the vegetables that are popular, as well as some that are not as popular but just as delicious.

Potatoes

China and India are now the world's biggest potato producers. Asia and Europe are the world's major potato-producing regions, accounting for more than 80 percent of world production in 2006. The United Kingdom is the eleventh-largest potato-producing country. In Britain, people consume ninety-four kilograms of potatoes per person per year. Potatoes fight hunger!

Some Interesting Facts about the Development of the Potato

1570: The potato arrives in Europe.
1609: European sailors take the potato to China.
1719: Potatoes arrive in the United States.
1801: The first French fries are served in America.
1845: The potato famine occurs in Ireland.
1853: The potato crisp is invented in New York.
1952: Mr. Potato Head toy is invented.
1995: The potato is grown in space.
2008: Year designated International Year of the Potato by the United Nations.

Potatoes are the number-one ingredient to have in your store cupboard. They contain vitamin C, fiber, and other nutrients, so many meals can be made from the humble potato. I have included some recipes later in this book.

When buying potatoes, go for a two-kilogram bag rather than a very large one. With larger bags, by the time you get to the bottom, most of the potatoes have gone bad or sprouted roots, so buy smaller amounts unless you have a very large family. It is best to buy potatoes loose or in paper sacks. If plastic is used for packaging, remove the wrapper when you get home, as plastic makes the item sweat. Potatoes shouldn't be refrigerated. Store them at room temperature with plenty of ventilation.

King Edward, Desiree, Maris Piper—these varieties are excellent for roasting and making fries. Wilja is good for mashing, Estima and Marfona are suitable for baking, and Charlottes are for salads. If you can't obtain a certain variety, go for the all-rounder.

Onions

Onions have been an important part of our diet since the beginning of civilization. The onion is believed to have originated in Asia, though it is likely that onions may have grown wild on every continent.

Onion lovers around the world know that this versatile vegetable can be cooked and eaten in many ways. It is another vegetable suitable for your "five a day."

Know Your Onions!

English onions are quite strong compared with some species grown in Europe, so it is really a matter of taste.

There is such a lot you can do with an onion—fry, bake, or boil. Most savory dishes contain onion in the ingredients.

Yellow: Yellow onions are for general use. Very small ones can be used for pickling.

White: Small white onions or cocktail onions can be pickled in plain white vinegar.

Red: Red onions have a mild to sweet flavor. You can use them to make onion rings or add them to salads.

Leeks: Leeks are related to onions. Wash them well, slice them up, and add them to stews or roast. Small new leaks can be steamed, seasoned, and rolled in butter.

Shallots: Shallots have a mild, sweet flavor. They can be cooked whole in casseroles and stews. They can also be added to sautéed potatoes with a clove or two of garlic. They grow in clusters like garlic; many bulbs come from one plant.

Note: The above varieties should be stored at room temperature and will remain fresh for two to three weeks. If you grow your own, string them up and store them in a dry shed.

Spring onions (scallions): Scallions can be chopped up and sprinkled over salads. They should be stored in the fridge (in the crisper/salad box).

Onion Johnnies

Years ago, French farmers, generally from Brittany, came to England once a year carrying strings of onions on their bicycles to sell door to door. This tradition was very popular, and housewives at the time looked forward to these visits. The onions these farmers sold were smooth and mild and had a pinkish color. At the port of Roscoff in Brittany, there is a museum in their honor. Good news: I think the onion Johnnies are making a comeback. I was recently given a string of delicious onions by my daughter-in-law. She said she bought them from an Onion Johnny.

Greens

Brussels Sprouts

It was probably the Romans who first cultivated a small cabbage similar to a sprout. Brussels sprouts as we know them date back to around the thirteenth century in areas around Belgium and Holland and in cooler parts of northern Europe. French settlers brought them to the United States in the eighteenth century. Today Britain and the Netherlands grow equal amounts, but Britain doesn't export them as much. They tend to enjoy Brussels sprouts in the winter after the frost. They are a firm favorite on the Christmas menu.

Brussels sprouts will store well in a cool larder for about ten days. You can also buy them frozen. If you live on your own or with a partner, fresh is better, as you can buy in small amounts as needed.

Savoy Cabbage

Savoy cabbage is a firm, wrinkled-leaf winter cabbage. It is delicious and goes a long way. Savoy cabbage that has been cooked, chopped up, and sprinkled with lemon juice is known as January King. Savoy cabbage can be stored in a cool place up to four or five days or longer in the salad compartment of the fridge.

Broccoli

Broccoli provides more than thirty milligrams of vitamin C per helping, plus dietary fiber, and it has anticancer compounds. Try not to boil broccoli too much, as this destroys some of the nutrients. Instead, you can stir-fry or steam it. Broccoli should be stored in the salad compartment of the fridge, but it does not keep for long. Eat it fresh if possible.

Kale and Spring Greens

Kale and spring greens are very high in nutrients, like other greens. These vegetables should be stored in a cool place or a crisper (salad box).

Carrots

Believe it or not, carrots come in different colors. Get a hold of a seed catalog, and you will be surprised by the varieties. Farmers' markets may stock a variety, but you will likely need a vegetable plot or a window box to grow some of them, as they don't seem readily available in the shops.

All carrots should be stored in a cool, dry place. If your carrots suddenly go black, don't throw them away. If you keep them for a week or two, sometimes the starch rises to the top and discolors the outside. Use a speed peeler, and you'll soon see how lovely and orange the flesh is underneath.

I encourage you to try all different vegetables. Below is a small list of a few you may enjoy.

Sweet Potatoes: Sweet potatoes have lovely orange flesh. Peel them, chop them up, and put them in a freezer bag with rosemary and garlic to use with roasted vegetables.

Yams: Yams can be bought in supermarkets specializing in West Indian and Asian food. Your greengrocer may also be able to get you one to try. They have a hard, rough skin, but the flesh is white and can be mashed like that of a potato when cooked. Yams have a slightly nutty flavor.

Peppers: Peppers can be stuffed with chili mincemeat, wrapped in tinfoil, and frozen. Stuffed peppers make a nice midweek meal. Try boiled rice or salad with them.

Asparagus: If you're not an expert, cook asparagus for two or three minutes in boiling water. When the stalks are just tender, drain them and toss them in salted butter with a little pepper.

I have provided some vegetable recipes later in this book. Many are suitable as vegetarian meals, as I have added some protein to them by using ingredients such as beans.

Fruit

Take fruit out of plastic bags. If you buy from a shop or market stall that uses brown paper bags, it is OK to store the fruit in these for a couple of days. Mushrooms should *always* be put into paper bags. (Mushrooms also freeze well, by the way.)

Remember, fruit looks good in a fruit bowl and will more than likely be eaten!

MEAT

Beef

Beef has been on the menu since 8000 BC when cattle were first domesticated. This gave access to meat, milk, and leather.

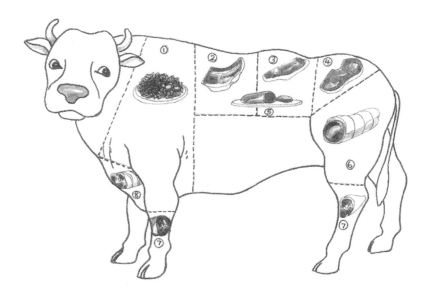

Now we enjoy it as roast beef, burgers, and steak. Beef can also be served in casserole or salted. Beef is a source of protein, iron, and eight vitamins.

Lamb

Lamb is one of the best-flavored meats. Roasted, grilled, or stewed—whichever way it is cooked, lamb is delicious.

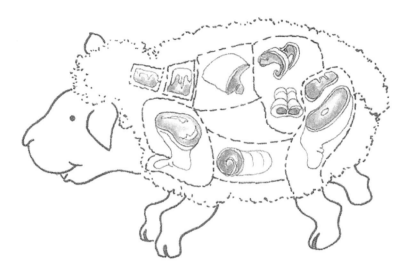

Lamb seems to be more expensive than other meats, but this doesn't have to be the case. If you visit your butcher, you can ask him or her for a cheaper cut.

Pork

Pork is one of the most economical meats you can buy. There is no waste—everything can be used, from the feet (trotter) to the pig's head.

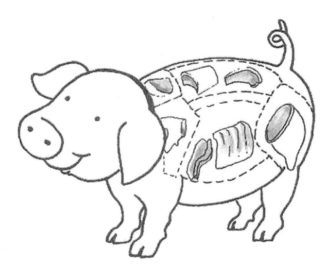

Some popular cuts of pork include leg, belly (one of the cheaper cuts, but delicious), shoulder, spare ribs, mince, brawn, ham, bacon, and trotter.

Poultry

Chicken

These days, chicken is inexpensive and ideal for a midweek roast. Any leftovers can be eaten cold the next day with salad.

Turkey

Don't just have turkey at holiday time. It is plentiful in the supermarket, cut into smaller joints. If you live alone or with a partner, turkey makes a lovely treat in place of other meats.

Duck

Duck is quite versatile—check out different recipes on the Web. I like roasted duck or a confit. It can also be used in Asian cooking or a spicy stir-fry.

Goose

Goose was once Britain's favored Christmas dish before the turkey that has now become standard. It is a very rich meat, so cooking it with fruit such as pear or cranberries is recommended to get the most from this bird.

Goose has the reputation of being greasy although this fat, when used to roast vegetables is delicious. If the skin on the outside is pricked with a fork the fat will run out into the roasting pan. It can then be used to roast potatoes and mixed vegetables of your choice.

FISH

*F*ish is at the top of the list when it comes to healthy eating, as it is full of essential oils. Some fish are under threat in our seas, so they must be protected. Other species, however, should be considered, as they are just as delicious. Here is a list of some of the fish we need to preserve.

- Cod
- Whitebait
- Hake
- Bluefin tuna
- Shark
- Skate
- Wild halibut
- Dover sole
- Sea bass
- Wild salmon

All fish is good to eat, so try some of these serving suggestions;

Sprat: Wash and dry the sprats. Heads can be removed or left on. Dust with seasoned flour, and fry lightly in a little oil until brown. Lay on paper towels to soak up any oil. Serve on a warm plate with fresh bread and butter.

Pollack: Pollack is a cousin of cod. Take the fillets and lightly fry, grill, or batter for fish and chips. Pollack is also good for fish cakes.

Pout: This can be prepared in the same manner as pollack.

Mackerel: Make sure the mackerel is very fresh. Take out the middle bone, and lay the fish flat. Wash and dry, lightly flour, and cook slowly in some oil until it is brown on both sides.

Serve with bread and butter and a little salad. You can always ask your fishmonger to fillet the mackerel.

Lemon sole: Lemon sole is a flat fish and can be eaten on the bone. Ask the fishmonger to prepare the fish for cooking, which includes removing any side bones and guts. Wash in salt water. Lay the fish onto a piece of tinfoil, and season with salt, pepper, lemon juice, and a handful of chopped parsley. Wrap the foil around the fish, and bake in a moderate oven for ten to twelve minutes. Serve with sauté potatoes and peas.

Black bream: Black bream is not a popular fish, but seek it out, as it is relatively inexpensive and has firm, sweet flesh. The fishmonger will descale and clean it. Bake in greaseproof paper or in tinfoil (as with the lemon sole).

Gray mullet: Gray mullet is best used for fish soup. Fillet the mullet, cut it into chunks, and add other fish, such as pollack, whiting, and smoked haddock. Stir in cooked (softened) onions, and simmer in a little water (just enough to cover) for ten minutes. Season and taste. Pour in three-quarters of a pint (500 mL) of milk. Mix a dessert spoon of cornstarch in a jug with a little milk or water, and pour into the soup to thicken. Cook on low heat so as not to burn, stirring throughout. Add herbs, such as fennel, dill, or parsley). Some precooked potatoes or thinly sliced carrots can be added as well. Serve with crusty bread.

Red gurnard: Red gurnard is an ugly fish, but it is delicious. It is suitable for fish stew, and it can be grilled as well. Once again, have a word with your friendly fishmonger.

Note: Always wash fish thoroughly and pat it dry with paper towels before cooking. All fish should be stored in a fridge or freezer until needed.

Dairy

Milk

These days, supermarkets stock many types of milk, although the most common is still cow's milk. Others include goat's milk and sheep's milk. For the lactose intolerant, there are plant-based substitutes, including soy, rice, oat, coconut, and almond milk.

Milk in the United Kingdom is distinguishable by its fat content:

- Whole or full-fat milk contains about 3.5 percent fat.
- Semi-skim milk contains about 1.7 percent fat.
- Skim milk contains 0.1 to 0.3 percent fat.

Skim and semi-skim milk contain less energy than full-cream milk, so they're not really suitable for children younger than two years.

Some supermarkets are now selling milk with 1 percent fat, which retains the creamy flavor of whole milk.

Butter

Butter has always been a winner, especially with its unique taste. In recent years, the general public has grown somewhat nervous about consuming butter because of its fat content. This is a pity, as certain spreads and margarines on the market are just as high in fat.

Look for butter made from the milk of organic grass-fed cows. As with most dairy products, you will notice the difference in taste when it comes to your cooking.

Cream

There is a variety of cream on the market, each with its own consistency and uses.

- Double cream
- Single cream
- Whipping cream
- Clotted cream
- Crème fraîche
- Ice cream
- Sour cream

Yogurt

Yogurt contains protein and vitamin B_2. Some yogurt contains living bacteria that are healthy to the digestive system (probiotics). Yogurt is easy to make at home, and I've included a recipe for you to try.

Say Cheese!

There are some very tasty cheeses on the market. Cheddar is a firm favorite, as it is versatile and good for cooking. Cheese on toast is a good standby for when people drop in unexpectedly. Try some red Leicester; it adds color to this simple meal.

Cheese shops are popping up in most towns. They stock many cheeses, both domestic and imported. Cheese is produced throughout the world and is available in a wide range of flavors and textures. It is made from the milk of cows, sheep, and goats.

There are some fine blue cheeses on the market; most are pungent, especially stilton, gorgonzola, and Roquefort). These are all acquired tastes, but if you try them, I am sure you will be pleasantly surprised.

Hard cheeses, such as cheddar, can be frozen. Parmesan cheese can even be grated while frozen.

It is essential to store all dairy products in the fridge. Butter, cheese, and milk can be put in the freezer if you have extra supplies.

Eggs

Chicken eggs are the most commonly eaten eggs. They are high in protein, vitamins A and B, and omega-3 fatty acids. There is so much to say about them. In addition to all the meals that are our favorites, eggs are included in the ingredients of cakes, puddings, biscuits, and sauces. There is always a meal that can be made when there are eggs in the cupboard.

Duck eggs are becoming more popular, and they make really good omelets. They are also used for making cakes, as they are far richer than chicken eggs. Duck eggs are nice boiled with bread and butter or hard-boiled with salad.

Quail eggs are often on the menus of fine-dining restaurants, and they can often be found at farmers' markets.

Eggs are safe to eat as long as they are properly cooked. This is especially important for young children and pregnant women.

As always, go for free-range eggs or organic if you can, it really makes a noticeable difference to the taste.

Eggs should be stored in a cool, dry place—not in the refrigerator.

Fridge Storage

As mentioned in previous sections, here is a summary of my fridge storage tips.

- Put all meat and dairy products into the fridge as soon as you receive a delivery or return home from shopping.
- Make sure that food is in good condition and fresh when it is delivered.
- Make sure the fridge is cleaned regularly. Put all raw meat at the bottom of the fridge so blood and other juices don't contaminate cooked produce. Keep all food covered, especially meat.
- If room permits, put food in sealed containers so different odors don't mix.
- Position cheese and dairy products at the top of the fridge, with cooked meats and pies below.
- In most fridges, salads should be stored in the crisper at the bottom of the fridge; however, it is safer to use a large plastic container to store salad above the raw meat. Wash all salad thoroughly before use.
- Don't overfill your fridge. Make sure air flows between items.
- If you need to split a packet, freeze the unused portion if it is not to be used within twenty-four hours.
- Put items in the fridge to thaw overnight.

Freezer Storage

- To keep food frozen during transportation, have it delivered (if possible), or use a freezer bag or box. Remove all old food from the freezer and discard.
- Cover food in the freezer using either plastic boxes or freezer bags. If you buy fresh meat or fish to freeze, first separate it into individual portions, and store these in freezer bags. This will save you time later.
- Cooked meat freezes very well. Slice meat up, store it in individual plastic boxes, and label. A box can be thawed out overnight in the fridge for sandwiches the next day.
- Keep the freezer clean at all times. Don't let odd bits of food lay in the bottom.

Food That Freezes Well

Cheese, butter, milk, mushrooms, leftovers, and green vegetables all freeze well. (I don't blanch my vegetables—I think blanching spoils the taste and texture.) Cabbage can be frozen, but frozen cabbage must be dropped into boiling water to cook. Thus it is a good idea to wash it and cut it up before freezing.

Always have boiling water ready to put the frozen food in to cook.

Herbs and Spices

Allspice was found on the island of Jamaica by Christopher Columbus and is used a lot in Jamaican cooking. It is also used in cake making in the United Kingdom and sausage making in Germany.

Anise has a sweet flavor with a hint of licorice. It is used in British aniseed balls.

Basil is originally from India but is best known in Italian cuisine. Fresh basil is best, and you can buy little pots from the supermarket. Basil should be torn rather than chopped; tearing releases the oils and aroma. Add basil to tomatoes when making pesto sauce. Try purple basil—it's stronger and great in Thai food.

Bay leaf has a distinct flavor and aroma. Add it to flavor stews and casseroles, but remove it before serving, as it is tough.

Caraway also has a strong, distinct flavor. It can be added to curries or used to make seedcake.

Cardamom has a fruity, warm flavor. It can be used with sweet dishes.

Coriander works well with fish and poultry. It can be purchased in little pots and should be crushed with a pestle and mortar. You can also buy seeds ground or whole. Coriander is an acquired taste!

Chili comes in many forms. I favor dried, as you can take one or two dried chilies and sprinkle them over a dish, which gives you more control. Fresh chilies must be chopped. For this process, I advise you to wear rubber or plastic gloves. At the very least, thoroughly wash your hands after handling them.

Chives have an oniony flavor and are nice chopped up and sprinkled over baked potatoes and omelets.

Cloves: I use a lot of these. I always use the little round top, which holds all the spice, instead of putting the whole clove in the dish. This way you don't end up with a clove in your mouth later. Ground cloves are easier to work with, and you need just a pinch. Add cloves to hot toddies, apple pies, and of course curry.

Curry powder is already blended. Try to blend your own spices if you have them. It makes a better curry. There are some good jars of curry sauce on the market nowadays and are great for time saving.

Cinnamon is a lovely spice, mostly used in cake making. It is very aromatic. It is popular in Persian cuisine but is also nice in buns, pickles, and apple pie.

Cumin has a smoky and earthy flavor, like curry.

Celery is mostly used as a vegetable although I often use celery as an herb, the stalks are eaten in salads, and the crown can be braised. Celery makes a lovely addition to many soups.

Dill works well with fish. If you have a whole fish, ask your fishmonger to clean it up. Put a handful of chopped dill in the body of the fish, and add half a stick of butter, a squeeze of lemon juice, and salt and pepper. Wrap in tinfoil or greaseproof paper, and slowly bake for about thirty-five minutes.

Dried herbs: You can obtain a good range of dried herbs these days. The little bottles look very attractive on the kitchen counter.

Ginger has a range of uses, and it is very warming. Ground ginger can be sprinkled on melon, stem ginger is good for sweet dishes, and root ginger (peeled) is great in Chinese food. Ginger is also good with ice cream.

Lemongrass has a citrus flavor. To use, discard the tough outer layer, and chop finely. You might also put a couple of stalks in the water of a fish kettle for a fresh, lemony taste.

Mint is one of the favorites. Add it to new potatoes and roast lamb, or make mint tea or mint sauce.

English mustard should be used sparingly, as it is quite hot. It is very good on ham, chicken, and roast beef. Dried mustard powder can be mixed with water and made up as you need it. You can also add a small amount of it to oil and vinegar for a salad dressing.

Dijon mustard (French mustard) isn't quite so hot, but it is full of flavor. I like it on pork or duck. Try it!

Nutmeg is sweet and aromatic. Grate it over baked rice pudding or egg custard.

Oregano is mainly used in pasta dishes. It is also popular in Turkish cuisine, especially for the flavoring of meat dishes like kebabs.

Paprika is made from red pepper. It can be added to soups and stews.

Parsley can be made into a sauce to top a piece of whitefish. It is also nice with boiled ham and new potatoes. You can chew a sprig of parsley to freshen your breath.

Poppy seeds can be sprinkled on homemade bread before baking. They can also be used in cakes.

Rosemary is great with lamb. It is also good finely chopped and added to potatoes before roasting. Try a little garlic with it.

Salt comes in several varieties. Table salt is quite high in sodium. Sea salt is good for cooking, but be wary—it is quite strong. Rock salt can be used in a grinder.

Sage is good with chicken and pork.

Saffron is a very expensive spice that comes from the autumn crocus. Saffron cake is popular in Cornwall. It turns rice yellow and is used in many Asian dishes.

Tarragon is good with lamb or chicken. Chop the tarragon, mix it with butter, and rub the mixture under the skin of a chicken before roasting for a nice treat.

Thyme is good with beef and chicken.

Vanilla is very versatile and is used in cakes, puddings, custards, and pears. Vanilla can be bought as an essence or in pods. Pods are quite strong, so fill a jar with sugar and add a pod; it will flavor the sugar, which can then be used for making cake or crème brûlée.

Vinegar comes in several varieties. Malt vinegar is an important ingredient; in my opinion, it is the only vinegar for fish and chips. Wine and cider vinegars can be used to make salad dressings. Balsamic vinegar, a product of Italy, can also be used as a salad dressing.

Watercress has a lovely hot flavor and can be grown in pots on a windowsill. Use in salads or to make watercress soup.

OILS

Olive Oil

*O*live oil is divided into four main groups, each distinguished by its level of acidity.

Extra-virgin olive oil is the highest-quality olive oil, made from the first pressing of the olives, and it has the lowest acidity. It is manually cold pressed, without the use of heat or chemicals, so the oil is not altered. This type of olive oil is best for making salad dressing and drizzling over tomatoes and fresh basil leaves.

Virgin olive oil is made in the same way as extra-virgin olive oil. It has acidity of less than 2 percent and can be used in the same way as extra-virgin olive oil.

Olive oil, also known as pure olive oil, has 3.3 percent acidity. It can be used in cooking.

Light olive oil is made from a filtered combination of refined olive oil, with small amounts of virgin olive oil. Despite its name, it has the same number of calories as other oils. *Light* refers to its texture and taste. It ideal for baking and, because it has a high smoking point, can be used for deep-frying.

Cooking Oils

Sunflower oil is used for cooking and is ideal for salad dressings and chips.

Rapeseed oil is a great British alternative to olive oil.

I have only listed a couple of oils, but I encourage you to read the labels and try different types. Supermarkets are well stocked. Look for the smoking point, and also look to see whether the oil is saturated or unsaturated. A high smoking point is best for higher-temperature frying, and saturated fats can be extremely unhealthy if overused. Change the oil in your fryer at regular intervals. Old oil is very bad for you.

Basic Kitchen Equipment

Fruit bowl: If people see fruit in a bowl on show, they are more likely to eat it.

Kitchen food thermometer: This is an essential piece of equipment for cooking meat and warming liquid to the correct temperature.

Kitchen scales: You can buy these cheaply.

Kitchen scissors: Use these for cutting around fish, pies, and the like. They are also helpful for opening tough food packets.

Liquidizer/Blender: This appliance is ideal for making soups and baby food.

Mixing bowls (plastic, metal, ceramic, glass)

Pie dishes

Ramekins: Use these for small puddings, soufflés, and soft chocolate sponges.

Pans: You should have an eight-inch saucepan, a six-inch saucepan, two smaller saucepans for milk, eggs, and sauces, one very large saucepan, one large frying pan, and one small omelet pan.

Sieves: Buy good-quality stainless-steel sieves. Cheap ones will rust.

Slow cooker: A slow cooker with a removable ceramic bowl is a must. Fill with your favorite food (e.g., chicken, lamb, beef, bacon joints), vegetables, a couple of stock cubes, and a handful of herbs. Cover with water, switch on, and leave. When you get home from work, college, or a day out, your meal will be ready to eat. No hassle.

Small microwave: A microwave is not essential, but one is useful if you live alone. Don't use it instead of an oven; use it only for little jobs (e.g., defrosting or warming up). Two items that lend themselves to a microwave oven are onions and fish.

Spoons (wooden spoons, spatulas, tablespoons, dessert spoons, teaspoons, soup ladle, slotted spoon, measuring spoons)

Steamer: This is an essential piece of equipment. It comes as a saucepan, with two or three slotted containers sitting on top of each other. This enables you to cook several vegetables at the same time. You can buy electric or nonelectric steamers.

Teapot: A medium-sized teapot should be sufficient for most households.

Tins:

Bun tins: You should have a twelve-cup tin and a six-cup tin.

Loaf tins

Round cake tins: If possible, buy tins with removable sides and loose bottoms.

Sponge tins: If possible, buy tins with loose bottoms. Two should be enough.

Vegetable rack: Vegetables keep better surrounded by air.

A lot of this equipment may be expensive to begin with. Make a list, and give it to friends and relatives. These items are good ideas for Christmas and birthday presents. You will probably be lucky enough to receive the finest-quality goods, and these will last a lifetime. People don't like to buy cheap products when giving a gift.

Hygiene

Take note of these simple rules for a hygienic kitchen.

- Always wash your hands before handling food.
- Use different chopping boards for vegetables, raw meat, and bread. Keep the chopping boards for specific items separate by color-coding them. Colored boards can be a bit pricey, but shop around—it's worth the effort.
- Store food at the correct temperature. If your fridge is not cold enough, food can spoil.
- Check the expiration date.
- Store cooked meat away from uncooked meat. Uncooked meat should be placed on the bottom shelf, as juices may drip over other items in the fridge. It is better to store fresh meat in a dish until it is oven ready.
- Throw out faulty or damaged equipment. It may contain hidden bacteria that can contaminate food and cause food poisoning.
- Wash tea towels and dishcloths regularly.
- Wash your hands after touching high-risk foods such as eggs, raw meat, and chicken.
- Keep the fridge and freezer tidy and clean. Promptly wipe up any spills.
- Cover all food separately before you put it in the fridge or freezer. This stops different smells from blending and spoiling other flavors. Also, it's more hygienic.
- Wash vegetables and fruit before eating, as they often contain residue from sprays and insecticides. Also, fruit and vegetables are handled quite a bit.

Terms and Conversions

Abbreviations

Tbsp.	tablespoon
Dsp.	dessert spoon
tsp.	teaspoon
g	gram
kg	kilogram
cL	centiliter
mL	milliliter
dL	deciliter
L	liter
" (e.g., 2")	inches
' (e.g., 1')	feet
C or c	Celsius
F or f	Fahrenheit
oz.	ounce

lb.	pound
fl. Oz.	fluid ounces
pt.	pint
SR or S/R	self-rising (flour)

Imperial Conversion Charts

Weight

Ounces		Grams
1	-	28
2	-	57
4	-	113
8	-	227
12	-	340
14	-	397
16 (1.0 lb.)	-	454

Liquid

Pint(s)		Milliliters
¼	-	118
½	-	237
1	-	473
1½	-	709
1¾	-	828

Oven Temperatures

	Fahrenheit	Celsius	Gas Mark
Very cool	225°	107°	¼
	250°	121°	½
Cool	275°	135°	1
	300°	149°	2
Moderate	325°	162°	3
	350°	176°	4
Moderately hot	375°	191°	5
	400°	204°	6
Hot	425°	218°	7
	450°	232°	8
Very hot	475°	246°	9

Note: A "fan oven" reduces heat slightly.

THE CHRISTMAS STORE CUPBOARD

*Y*ears ago, people saved up and had a share-out just before Christmas. These people belonged to saving schemes run by the local butcher or grocer. Toy shops ran them, as did social clubs and pubs. People had to save a few coppers each week. They often had big families, and the man of the house, if he worked, didn't earn very much. Money was short for some folk, but if the women were thrifty, all could have a nice Christmas.

During the last weeks before Christmas, everyone was a busy making gift for his or her loved ones. With the little money they had, they would build up a store cupboard with things that might be going cheap in the market. This wasn't easy, as money could be tight and most savings clubs didn't pay out until Christmas Eve or the day before. Fortunately, the shops stayed open until quite late. Both my grandparents would stay up half the night, preparing.

My mother would tell me about when she was a child. Back then my gran would make Christmas puddings, and the family would all join her in the kitchen. Into the mixture she would put silver three penny bits that she had saved up throughout the year. They would all stand in line to have a stir and make their wish. Then she would fill the pudding basins with the mixture, wrapping them up in greaseproof paper and old sheeting that had been boiled for the purpose, and steam them for about five hours.

Today you can buy excellent puddings from your local store. But I'm sure those old ones tasted wonderful.

Starting around the end of October, make room in your store cupboard. Each time you do your shopping, add one or two items that can be put away. You might use the following items during the festive season: flour, sugar, tea, coffee, mincemeat (for mince pies), biscuits, sweets, cream crackers, pickled onions, red cabbage, piccalilli, gherkins, tins of fruit, jellies, instant whip, custard powder, and sponge fingers. In addition, dripping and goose fat can be bought at the butcher's. Sausage meat and small, thin sausages will keep in the freezer, so these can be bought at a later date. Dairy products and fresh fruits and vegetables can be bought Christmas week. Make sure you save enough room to store them.

Don't forget the Christmas cake (see recipe).

A bottle of wine or spirits can be bought at intervals and stored in a cupboard as well. Beer can also be bought for storing.

For a New Year's resolution, buy a sealed money box, and try and save one pound a day (or whatever you can afford). It soon adds up.

Some Easy Recipes
USEFUL RECIPES

Soups

French Onion Soup

Vegetable Soup and Minestrone

Celery Soup

Watercress Soup

Cheesy Recipes

Easy Cheese on Toast

Cheese Sauce

Cauliflower and Macaroni and Cheese

Easy Puddings and Homemade Breakfasts

Junket

Creamy Yogurt

Rice Pudding

Porridge Oats

Muesli

Flapjacks

Meat Recipes

Pig's Trotter

Belly Pork

Hot Dogs

Steak and Kidney Pudding or Pie

Quarter Pounder (Easy Beef Burgers)

Chunky Oven Fries

Corned Beef Hash

Cheap and Easy Recipes

Lamb Hot Pot

Sauté Potatoes with Bacon and Sausage

Whitefish and Tasty Mash

Mediterranean Chicken Stir-Fry with Potatoes

Mincemeat

Dauphinoise Potatoes

Puddings and Cakes

Upside-Down Cake

Custard

Quick Trifle

Posh Custard

Applesauce

Salad Dressing

Green-Tomato Chutney

Easy Christmas Cake

French Onion Soup (serves 5_6)

This is a meal in itself.

1 Tbsp. olive oil
1 Tbsp. butter for frying
4 or 5 white onions, chopped
1 L warm water
3 beef-stock cubes (or veggie cubes for vegetarians)
½ cup white wine or sherry
1 tsp. dried thyme (or a handful of fresh thyme)
1 fresh garlic clove, chopped
Salt and pepper to taste
French bread (baguette)
Grated cheese to top bread (gruyère, cheddar)

Put the chopped onions into a large frying pan with olive oil and butter over a medium heat. Keep turning the onions so they cook evenly. Cook until golden brown. Transfer the onions into a large saucepan with the wine, thyme, garlic, and salt and pepper. Dissolve the beef-stock cubes in the warm water. Pour over mixture to fill the saucepan halfway. Cook soup slowly for about half an hour, or until onions are soft. While the soup is cooking, put bowls in the oven to warm. Lightly toast one side of the bread. Turn and add cheese. Toast the other side until the cheese has melted.

You may float the toasted bread on top of the soup; I prefer to keep it separate.

Vegetable Soup

Collect as many vegetables as you like (e.g., carrots, onions, celery, swede or turnip, and peas).

One clove of garlic (optional). Never overdo the garlic, as it can take over, masking the fresh taste of the vegetables.

Fill a large saucepan halfway with diced vegetables, add a good splash of olive oil, and cook on low heat until tender, stirring all the time. Add water or stock. Simmer for about half an hour. When the vegetables are tender, strain off liquid into a bowl or jug. Put the vegetables into a liquidizer for one quick blast; you don't want the vegetables too mushy. Return to the pan, and pour the liquid back over. Add a bay leaf and some fresh or dried herbs and salt and pepper. Stand overnight in a cool place or fridge. This gives the flavors chance to blend. Soup will be ready for lunch the next day.

Serve hot with crusty bread or croutons.

Note: Adapt this recipe for minestrone soup by adding two tablespoons of small macaroni, extra garlic, a tin of chopped tomatoes, a tin of butter beans, a tablespoon of tomato puree, and a level teaspoon of oregano. Serve with parmesan cheese and black pepper on top. Eat hot with chunks of crusty bread.

Celery Soup

1 Tbsp. olive oil
150 g (5½ oz.) celery, chopped
½ red onion, chopped
1 garlic clove, chopped
200 mL chicken or vegetable stock

Lightly heat the oil in a saucepan. Add the chopped onion, garlic, and celery, and cook over low heat until softened. While waiting, in a separate saucepan warm the stock over a medium heat. Once ready, pour the stock into the main pot along with the red onion, bring to a boil, and simmer for ten to twelve minutes. Take off heat and let cool for five minutes. In a bowl, blend with an electric hand blender or liquidizer. Pour back into the saucepan to bring back up to heat.

Serve with chunks of whole-wheat bread and fresh butter.

Watercress Soup

200 g (7 oz.) watercress, chopped
300 mL (½ pt.) vegetable stock, heated
25 g (1 oz.) butter
2 tsp. cornstarch, mixed to a paste with a little water
Salt and freshly ground pepper
Double cream to serve (optional)

Heat the butter on a medium heat until foaming. Add half of the watercress and all of the stock, and simmer for six to eight minutes. Add the cornstarch paste. Stir to combine. Season to taste with salt and freshly ground pepper. Add the remaining watercress, and stir to blend in.

Serve the soup in warm bowls. Garnish with a drizzle of double cream if you desire.

Cheesy Recipes

Easy Cheese on Toast

White or whole-wheat bread, sliced
Hard cheese (cheddar, red Leicester), thinly sliced
Butter or spread

*P*lace two or three slices of bread on wire rack of grill pan, and toast one side until golden brown. When done, place bread onto board, and butter uncooked side. Cover bread with sliced cheese, return to the grill pan, and toast until melted. Sliced tomatoes can be added before toasting.

Add Worcestershire sauce, delicious!

Cheese Sauce

140 g (5 oz.) cheddar cheese
Milk
Butter
1 Tbsp. cornstarch

Grate cheese onto a plate. Mix a tablespoon of cornstarch with a little cold milk until dissolved. Bring three-quarters of a pint of milk to a boil. Add knob of butter to the milk, and pour over the cornstarch mixture. Stir until thickened. Add the grated cheese and stir. Pour over your desired dish (e.g., cauliflower or macaroni).

Macaroni: Cook 130 g (4 oz.) macaroni in lightly salted boiling water until tender. Drain. Fill a glass pie dish halfway with the pasta. Pour the cheese sauce over the pasta, sprinkle some grated cheese on top, and bake in a moderate oven for about ten minutes, or until the cheese melts and is golden brown. This can be done under a grill, but you have to watch it.

Cauliflower: Use the same method as for macaroni.

Junket (serves 4)

1 pt. full-cream milk
1 level Tbsp. caster sugar
1 tsp. rennet
Grated nutmeg

Warm milk to 37°C (98°F). Stir in the sugar. Add the rennet. Stir in gently. Pour into a shallow dish and leave for an hour to an hour and a half in a warm place undisturbed until set. Chill in the refrigerator. Sprinkle with nutmeg.

Serve!

Creamy Yogurt (serves 4)
This simple homemade yogurt is rich and creamy.

400 mL rich, creamy milk (e.g., Channel Island or organic)
2 Tbsp. milk powder
100 mL single cream
3 Tbsp. live yogurt at room temperature

Warm the milk and cream to 46°C (115°F). Whisk in the milk powder until dissolved. Pour into a glass jug on top of the live yogurt, mix, and pour into a clean bowl. Cover and put into a warm airing cupboard and place a hot-water bottle beside it. Leave overnight. Pour into individual little pots with lids, or cover with plastic wrap. Transfer to fridge. It should last two or three days.

Traditional Baked Rice Pudding

Use a glass pie dish or casserole. Glass doesn't burn as quickly as metal.

2 Tbsp. pudding rice
1 Tbsp. sugar
1 pt. full-cream milk
1 Dsp. of butter
Nutmeg (optional)

Put pudding rice into a glass pie dish or small casserole. Add sugar and butter. Add the milk. Put onto the middle shelf of a moderate oven (160°C/320°F). After half an hour, give the pudding a stir to mix in the butter and sugar. Cook for at least two hours (maybe two and a half hours) until a dark-brown skin forms on top and the rice has absorbed all the milk, making it soft and creamy. If the skin is not browning, turn the temperature up a degree. The pudding can be cooked at the same time as a joint of meat or roast vegetables. You can add grated nutmeg to taste.

Quick Rice Pudding

3 Tbsp. pudding rice
Full-cream milk
Butter
1 Tbsp. Sugar

Put three tablespoons of pudding rice into a saucepan, and cover with water. Bring to a boil, and simmer for two minutes. Drain off the water, and put the rice back into the saucepan. Cover with full-cream milk, a knob of butter, a tablespoon of sugar, and a pinch of nutmeg. Bring to a boil. Turn down the heat, and simmer until the rice is soft and most of the milk is absorbed. Put the ingredients into an ovenproof dish, and keep warm in a low oven.

Serve with tinned apricots or peaches.

Porridge Oats

To make a lovely, creamy bowl of porridge takes no time at all.

2 cups fine-grain oats
2 cups full-cream milk
Large pinch of salt (sea or rock salt)

Put oats into a saucepan. Add milk and salt. Cook until the milk is hot and almost boiling. Stir continuously to prevent sticking or burning. It should thicken. Remove from the heat, still stirring. Pour into bowls.

Top with sugar, golden syrup, honey, or fresh fruit (e.g., bananas or apricots).

Microwave: Put oats, milk, and salt into a microwave-safe dish or glass bowl. Cook for two minutes, and then stir. Continue stirring until ready. It should take three to four minutes.

Muesli

1 cup oats
1 cup chopped nuts
1 handful mixed seeds

Mix all the ingredients. Add milk or eat dry. Put honey or maple syrup with the mixture if you like. Add fresh or dried fruit, nuts, raisins, dried apricots, or anything that takes your fancy.

A week's supply can be made and put into sealed plastic boxes for each day.

Flapjacks

350 g (12 oz.) porridge oats
175 g (6 oz.) butter
175 g (6 oz.) muscovado sugar
175 g (6 oz.) golden syrup
Zest of ½ lemon, finely grated
Pinch of ground ginger

Grease a flat baking tin with a little oil or butter. Line with greaseproof paper. Preheat oven to 150°C (300°F).

Melt butter over low heat in a medium pan. Add the syrup and sugar to butter, and heat gently. Once the sugar, syrup, and butter have all melted, remove from heat and stir in the oats, lemon zest, and ginger.

Pack the mixture into the baking tray, and squash down flat. Bake for forty minutes. When cooked, remove from the oven, cool for fifteen minutes, and then turn out onto a chopping board. Cut into squares.

Flapjacks are a delicious addition to a lunch box or a great grab-and-go breakfast.

Pork

Pig's Trotter

2 pig's trotters
Salt and pepper
Bay leaf
Onion
Carrot (optional)

Some of you may turn your nose up at the idea, but let me tell you this is one of the tastiest dishes to be found. Why not give it a try?

Ask your butcher to cut you off two medium-sized trotters. Place the trotters into a bowl of cold water for a couple of hours. Rinse thoroughly, place in a saucepan, and cover with cold water. Add bay leaf, onion, carrot, and salt and pepper. Bring to a boil, turn down the heat, and simmer for at least an hour and a half, until tender. Skim any residue from the top of the liquid. When cooked, lay on a warm plate and serve with freshly cooked carrots and onions and perhaps a dumpling or two.

Alternatively, serve cold with homemade piccalilli or your favorite chutney and freshly baked bread. Enjoy!

Note: The liquid used to cook the trotters in can be saved and used for a stew. When cool, strain and put in the freezer, if you have room.

Belly Pork

Pork stripes can be bought at the supermarket. These are delicious slowly roasted for a mid-week dinner.

You may also ask your butcher to cut off a piece of belly pork. Get him to score the top skin. The blade bone should be on the bottom for extra flavor. Make sure it is quite lean down the side of the joint.

Put in a roasting bag with a sprig of thyme and some chopped up apple skin and salt and pepper. Be very careful when removing the joint from the bag, as the liquid it accumulates is very hot. Strain the liquid and put it into a jug to be made into gravy. Place the joint onto a dry roasting tin. Add a little olive oil, and then put back into a hot oven for about half an hour to crisp up the cracking. When cooked, take out and lay on a carving board to rest. Cover with tinfoil.

Carve down and lay the strips on hot plates. Serve with loads of crispy roast potatoes.

Thicken the liquid saved from the meat with gravy granules, sauce thickening powder or cornstarch.

Dijon mustard is a good accompaniment.

Hot Dogs

Here is a quick recipe that can be used with a tin of hot dogs. Ideal food for a hungry mob after school, or a lunchtime snack.

Drain the hot dogs and rinse to get rid of most of the salt. Chop into small pieces.

Lightly fry an onion until soft. Add other vegetables (e.g., mushrooms, zucchini, or sweet red peppers), one clove of garlic, and tomatoes. Add hot dogs, and stir into vegetables. Add a little water or stock if it becomes too dry, but not too much. (Don't let the vegetables get soggy.) Spoon over mashed potatoes or boiled rice.

Chorizo or good sausages can also be used. Baked beans can be used instead of the vegetables. This option is good poured over mashed potatoes.

Alternatively, lay the hot dog in a long soft roll, and coat with fried onions, tomato ketchup, or mustard.

Steak and Kidney Filling

1 lb. good steak (rump or skirt)
½ lb. kidney, sliced
1 medium onion, diced
1 garlic clove (optional), diced
Salt and pepper to taste
Red wine
Sprig of fresh thyme or a pinch of dried thyme
1 bay leaf
Cornstarch or gravy powder for thickening

Cover the steak with half a glass of red wine, and place in the fridge overnight. Drain off wine and pat with paper towels before preparing to cook. Slice the steak into small pieces and put into a bowl. Add a little olive oil to rub into the meat. Season. Heat frying pan until quite hot, and put in the steak. Fry until just brown to seal the outside. Stir well to avoid burning. Put back into a warm bowl, and put aside. Add onion, garlic, and kidney to the frying pan with a little olive oil. Cook until soft. Put all the ingredients into a saucepan. Add water and a spoonful of flour to cover. Bring to a boil, and then turn down the heat. Mix well, and simmer for one to two hours, or until tender. Watch closely, as it may run out of water. Top off from time to time to keep the meat covered. Remove bay leaf. Mix a level tablespoon of gravy granules or stock cube, and add to the saucepan. The broth should thicken nicely. Stir well. Turn off the heat, and set the saucepan aside. The filling is now ready to be used for a pie or pudding.

Suet dough

225 g (8 oz.) self-rising flour
60 g (2 oz.) beef or vegetarian suet
Ice-cold water

Put flour into a bowl, and mix in the suet. Add cold water a little at a time until the dough comes together. Don't make it too wet. Knead the dough lightly for about one minute, adding flour to the board. To make this into a pie, roll out the dough and line a pudding basin or pie dish; add the filling of your choice and put aside to cool. Fill a basin or pie dish three-quarters of the way with the filling. Make lids for both, and make sure the edges are sealed.

Pudding

Cover the top of the basin with greaseproof paper.

Wrap pudding basin in tinfoil and a clean square of cotton material. Tie at the top, making a handle for easy lifting. Place in a large saucepan, fill halfway with water, and cover with lid. Bring to a boil, and simmer for an hour and a half. Top off regularly with water, ensuring it does not boil dry. When cooked, remove from the saucepan, and stand until cool enough to remove the material and foil. Loosen edges of the pudding with a knife, and place a plate upside down on the basin. Carefully turn out the pudding onto the plate. Heat up the rest of the gravy, and pour over the pudding.

Pie

Crimp the edges of the pie, and then make a hole in the center at the top to allow any steam to escape. Bake in a hot oven until light golden brown. Brush egg wash onto the top, and put back in hot oven for five minutes.

Suet Dumplings

Prepare the pudding dough, but add more water. Dumplings should be too damp to handle. Spoon into the stew.

Very light!

Quarter Pounders (Easy Beef Burgers)

450 g (1 lb.) good-quality ground beef
1 small onion, finely chopped
1 tsp. mixed herbs
1 Tbsp. vegetable oil
4 burger buns

Mix the beef, onion, and herbs in a bowl. Divide the mixture into four. Dampen hands, and carefully roll the mixture into the size of tennis balls. Carefully press down with the palm of your hand to flatten into patties about three centimeters thick. Make sure all the burgers are the same thickness so they will cook evenly. Very carefully lift onto a flat plate or tin, and cover with plastic wrap. Place in the fridge for thirty minutes. Can be left overnight.

Heat a flat frying pan and brush some olive oil onto the surface. Lay the burgers in the pan, and cook slowly for five minutes. Carefully turn them to cook the other side. Repeat this action, and cook for an extra ten minutes. If you like your burgers well-done, cook for an extra minute. Take the burgers off the heat and let rest for a minute in a warm place. Cut open the bun, and lightly toast. Lay the burger inside the bun, and add relish, cheese, tomato ketchup, mustard, or your choice of accompaniment.

Can be placed in a warm oven, covered with foil, until ready to eat.

Chunky Oven Fries

These fries are good to place in the center of the table to have with the beef burgers.

2 or 3 medium to large potatoes (Desiree), cut into large chunks
Peanut oil or vegetable oil
Freshly ground sea salt and black pepper

Put potatoes in a saucepan of cold water. Bring to a boil, and cook for two minutes. Strain off the water, and dry the potatoes on a kitchen towel. Spread evenly on a baking tin. Drizzle with oil so all fries are coated. Put in a very hot (220°C) oven to cook. Turn over twice during the cooking process, until golden brown. Take out of the oven or fryer, place on some kitchen paper to absorb access oil.

Serve in a basket, in the center of the table.

Season with sea salt, black pepper, and lots of malt vinegar.

Corned Beef Hash

Here is a quick, easy, and inexpensive meal for midweek or when people descend upon you unexpectedly; it only takes about ten minutes.

1 large tin of corned beef (keep tin in the fridge, the contents will slide out easier after opening), chopped
1 small onion, diced
2 small potatoes, diced
2 tomatoes, chopped
1 garlic clove (optional), diced
1 beef stock cube. Make a cup of stock that may be needed to moisten dish.
1 handful fresh parsley (optional), chopped

Open a tin of corned beef. Be very careful not to cut yourself, as the tin is very sharp. Use a cloth. Place potatoes, onions, and garlic in a large frying pan. Add a little oil, and cook slowly until golden brown. Add to the pan the tomatoes and corned beef. Carefully mix all the ingredients together. Add a little warm stock if needed, but the tomatoes should keep it moist. Mix in parsley if desired.

Eat with crusty French bread with fresh butter and a glass of red wine of your choice.

Note: Sweet potatoes can be used instead of regular potatoes, with zucchini and mushrooms.

Cheap and Easy Recipes

Lamb Hot Pot

450 g (1 lb.) neck of lamb
4 potatoes
2 carrots
1 small turnip or swede
1 stick of celery
1 small onion
1 handful mixed pulses
1 handful pearl barley
½ cup of butter beans, soaked
2 stock cubes
1 Tbsp. tomato puree
1 Dsp. mixed herbs (fresh or dried)
½ cup frozen peas (optional)
Salt and pepper

Dice up the meat and vegetables ready for the pan. Heat a large saucepan until very hot. Add some oil or beef dripping to the pan, add the lamb, and cook until brown on both sides. Add the vegetables, herbs, stock cubes, and some warm water to cover the ingredients. Bring to a boil, reduce heat, and simmer for at least an hour and a half. Make up one pint of stock to add to the stew if the water reduces too much. Keep an eye on it, or transfer to a slow cooker. Season to taste. Skim off any fat that forms, or leave overnight for fat to harden to remove it in one piece. Ten minutes before serving, add a splash of Worcestershire sauce and add four suet dumplings.

Fill four bowls. Serve with crusty bread.

Note: The neck of lamb should cost about £4.50, the vegetables about £1.50, and the rest of the ingredients should be in your store cupboard.

Sauté Potatoes with Bacon and Sausage

Slice four medium cooked potatoes quite thickly, and set aside on a plate. Chop two rashers of bacon and three sausages. Fry the bacon and sausage in a little oil until cooked. Don't crisp the bacon too much at this stage. Remove onto a warm plate. Fry the potatoes in the bacon fat until brown, and add the bacon and sausage back into the pan to crisp. Serve on hot plates with a poached egg and hot toast.

Have for breakfast or tea.

Whitefish And Tasty Mash

4 large potatoes, cut into quarters
1 small garlic clove, grated
½ tsp. French mustard
1 pack of whitefish fillets from the supermarket or 4 fillets of pollack from the fishmonger
1–2 sprigs of fresh parsley
½ cup milk
30 g (1 oz.) butter
Salt and pepper

Put potatoes into a saucepan of cold water. Add garlic (optional), and bring to the boil. Simmer until soft. Cook the garlic in with the potatoes to reduce potent flavor. Cover fish fillets in greaseproof paper after adding salt and pepper, chopped parsley, and a little milk. Put the wrapped fillets onto a flat dish and cook in a moderate oven for twenty minutes. Drain the potatoes and put back on the heat for one minute. Add a little milk and butter to warm. Mash well to get rid of lumps, and beat with wooden spoon, adding a little French mustard. Open the fish, and lay on hot plates with the mashed potato.

Serve with peas or spinach and a slice of lemon on the side. Sprinkle with chopped parsley (optional).

Mediterranean Chicken Stir-Fry With Potatoes

2 chicken breasts, cut into strips
500 g (1 lb.) new potatoes
1 small onion, chopped

½ pepper, sliced
1 zucchini, sliced
1 garlic clove, chopped
1 Tbsp. tomato puree
1 tsp. mixed herbs or oregano
Salt and pepper

Put potatoes into cold water, lightly salt, and bring to a boil. Turn down and simmer. When done, slice thickly and put onto a warm plate. Heat the pan or wok, and add a little oil. Put in the vegetables and chicken, and stir-fry until cooked. Add the potatoes. Mix tomato puree, salt and pepper, and herbs with a little water, and stir into the mixture.

Serve on hot plates with garlic bread and a glass of red wine (optional).

Note: The chicken breasts can be bought fresh. The rest of the ingredients should be in the cupboard or fridge.

Mincemeat

2 kg (5 lb.) ground beef or lamb
2 cups frozen mixed vegetables
1 small onion, chopped
1 garlic clove, chopped or grated
3 stock cubes

Put all ingredients into a large saucepan. Cover with water and bring to a boil. Simmer for one hour. Take any impurities or fat from the top, or wait until cold and lift any fat off. Tip the mixture into a colander, and collect the liquid drained in a large jug. Transfer the mixture into individual plastic containers, preferably about four. Put the gravy collected in the jug into a saucepan, and thicken with beef-gravy granules. Pour a little into each dish. When cool, put on the airtight lids and freeze. This will make four ready meals you can take out when you need mince.

Flavor and season to whatever dishes you are making.

Dauphinoise Potatoes

The ultimate plate of potatoes, great for vegetarians!

If you use cheese, you don't need anything else to accompany this dish.

Use all-rounders, Desiree, or King Edward potatoes.

500 g (1 lb.) potatoes
200 mL double cream
100 mL milk
1 garlic clove, crushed
50 g gruyère cheese (optional), grated
nutmeg (optional)

Preheat the oven to 180°C (350°F). Peel and slice potatoes very thinly, and place them into a bowl of cold water to stop them from browning. Rise and pat dry with paper towels. Place the cream, milk, and garlic into a saucepan, and bring to a gentle simmer. Add the potatoes to the milk mixture, and cook for about ten minutes until potatoes are tender and can be easily skewered with a fork. The starch in the potatoes should thicken the milk. Add a little grated nutmeg at this stage if desired. Transfer to a buttered ovenproof dish, and sprinkle with the grated cheese. Bake for about twenty-five minutes, until golden brown.

Serve on a hot plate.

Note: A little broccoli or spinach could accompany this dish, but with the cheesiness, it doesn't need much else…except, of course, a glass of chardonnay!

Puddings and Cakes

Upside-Down Cake

Heat the oven to 160°C (320°F)

Topping

50 g (1½ oz.) butter, softened
50 g (1½ oz.) soft light-brown sugar
7 pineapple rings in syrup (save the syrup to use in the cake mixture)
Glacé cherries (or tinned)

Cake

100 g (3½ oz.) butter, softened
100 g (3½ oz.) golden caster sugar
100 g (3½ oz.) plain flour
Pinch of salt
1 tsp. baking powder
1 tsp. vanilla extract
2 eggs

Beat the butter and sugar until creamy. Spread over the bottom and halfway up the side of a round (20–21 centimeters) cake tin. Arrange pineapple rings on top. Place the cherries in the center of the rings.

Put the cake ingredients into a bowl, adding two tablespoons of pineapple syrup. Beat to a soft consistency with an electric whisk. Spoon on top of pineapple and level.

Bake for thirty-five minutes. Leave to stand for five minutes. Turn out onto a plate. While it's still warm, serve with ice cream or crème fraîche.

Custard

There are many recipes for how to make the perfect custard, but if you have a tin of Bird's Custard Powder in your store cupboard, you can't go wrong.

Even the instant custard powder that sells for only a few pennies is great for quickness, but use full-cream milk instead of water.

Quick Trifle

Empty tin of oranges into a dish, and cover with orange jelly. Use half of the water (stated on the packet). When set, cover with instant custard made with milk.

Ladyfingers can be used in the jelly, but I find it more refreshing without.

Posh Custard

5 egg yolks
1 whole egg
1 vanilla pod
120 g (4 oz.) caster sugar
250 mL full-cream milk
250 mL double cream

Scrape the seeds from the vanilla pod into a saucepan, and then add the pod. Add milk. Bring to a boil, and then leave to stand. Whisk all the eggs and sugar together until pale and thick. Whisk in the vanilla-infused milk. Strain into a clean saucepan and put back on the lowest heat, stirring continuously until the custard thickens.

Now stir in the double cream and enjoy!

This custard is nice poured over fruitcake or pantone. Or serve it over slices of bread and butter sprinkled with raisins and almond flakes and baked for about ten minutes.

Applesauce

Bramley apples are good for this recipe, as they soften quicker, but any apple will do.

Peel apples and chop into slices. Put into a saucepan of water with some lemon juice to keep the flesh from discoloring. Save the skin. Rinse apples and cook in a small amount of water until soft (takes about three to four minutes). Drain through a sieve. Now put into sterilized jars. Don't make great amounts, as it doesn't last that long. Seal and store in the fridge for about one month.

You notice I haven't added any sugar to the apple. Sugar is optional. I find it is not needed with sweet, succulent pork.

Apple skins: Plunge these in lemon water to stop discoloration and clean. Drain and dry off, and then chop very finely and put the chopped skins into plastic bags or boxes. Put into the freezer. Keep for flavoring (e.g., sprinkle onto meat or puddings before cooking).

Salad Dressing

1 tsp. mustard powder
1 small garlic clove or 1 tsp. dried garlic
1 or 2 dried chilies
2 Tbsp. extra-virgin olive oil
2 Tbsp. white-wine or white-balsamic vinegar

Crush garlic, chilies, and mustard powder together. Transfer to a large jug, pour in oil, and stir. Add the vinegar. Make this about half an hour before serving, or leave overnight to fuse the flavors. Mix and strain, pour over salad.

This dressing can be made in larger quantities and stored. Adjust the amount of ingredients to suit, and then pour into sterilized bottles and seal until needed.

Shake before use.

Sterilization: Wash bottles and jars in hot, soapy water, or put in a dishwasher. Make sure they are sparkling clean. Now put into an oven at 140°C (280°F) for thirty minutes. Fill with your favorite preserve. To seal, lay a small paper disc on top. (These can be bought from a cookware shop.) I always put plastic wrap over the opening and then screw the top on tightly; this helps to seal it. When all the jars are filled, find a baking tray for the jars to stand on. Cool and serve.

Green-Tomato Chutney

There is no need to make loads of chutney, jam, or marmalade. In fact, it is easier and smarter to make smaller quantities a couple of jars at a time. It is essential to make sure your jars are spotlessly clean. After thoroughly washing your jars, pour boiling water into them. Put in a teaspoon in each prevent cracking, and let the jars sit for a few minutes before carefully pouring out the water and allowing them to dry. Then put into a warm oven for twenty minutes.

This recipe will make a couple of jam jars' worth.

900 g (2 lb.) tomatoes, mixed green and red, halved
3 onions, roughly chopped
90 g (3 oz.) raisins
250 g (9 oz.) light muscovado sugar
1 medium-hot red chili
1 tsp. salt
2 tsp. yellow mustard seeds
300 mL white-wine vinegar

Put the green tomatoes together with the onions in a large stainless-steel or enameled pan with the raisins, sugar, chili, salt, mustard seeds, and vinegar. Bring to a boil. Turn down the heat, and leave to simmer for an hour, giving the occasional stir to reduce the risk of the chutney sticking. After about twenty-five minutes, add the red tomatoes and continue to simmer. Leave to cool and then spoon into sterilized jars and seal.

Easy Christmas Cake

225 g (8 oz.) plain flour
200 g (7 oz.) dark-brown sugar
200 g (7 oz.) butter
800 g (1¾ lb.) mixed dried fruit
150 g (5 oz.) glacé cherries, halved
100 g (3oz.) almonds, halved
¼ tsp. salt
½ tsp. mixed spice
½ tsp. ground cinnamon
2 Tbsp. black treacle
1 Tbsp. marmalade
¼ tsp. vanilla essence
1 small tin crushed pineapple
4 eggs (beaten)
4 Tbsp. brandy (optional)

Heat the oven to 150°C (300°F).

Grease a round (20 cm/8 in.) tin. Line the bottom and around the sides with greaseproof paper or parchment paper cut to size. Sieve the flour into a bowl. The spices and salt can be added to the flour at this stage. Crack the eggs into a basin and beat together. Add vanilla essence. Cream butter and sugar in a large mixing bowl. Add the treacle and marmalade. Mix in the eggs a little at a time, adding a couple of tablespoons of flour with the last amount. Fold in the remaining flour until well mixed. Add the dried fruit, glacé cherries, and chopped almonds. If the batter is a little dry, add the crushed pineapple until you are happy with the consistency. Turn the mixture into the prepared baking tin. Bake in the oven for three hours, and then test with a skewer. If not ready, bake for another hour, testing every twenty minutes until the skewer comes out clean.

Remove from the oven and leave to cool for twenty minutes. Turn out onto a wire rack. Remove all greaseproof paper. When the cake is cool, make a few holes in the top or bottom. Pour three or four tablespoons of brandy over the cake, and let it soak in.

Icing

Buy a pack of fondant icing. Roll it out and cover the cake. Use a little jam or marmalade to stick the icing to the cake. Trim the bottom edges when the cake is standing on a round cake board. Put a wide piece of ribbon around the bottom edge and secure. Decorate the top with a robin or a piece of holly. Rolled-out marzipan could be used to cover the cake before the icing.

Notes

Printed in Great Britain
by Amazon